modern
Grill & Garden

modern
Grill & Garden

Martha Gill

Photographs—Brad Newton
Chef—Shaun Doty
Garden Advice — Walter Reeves

LONGSTREET
Atlanta, Georgia

Published by LONGSTREET PRESS, INC.

A subsidiary of Cox Newspapers, a subsidiary of Cox Enterprises, Inc.

2140 Newmarket Parkway, Suite 122, Marietta, GA 30067

Printed in the United States of America

1st printing 1999

Library of Congress Catalog Card Number: 99-60104

ISBN: 1-56352-567-4

Digital film prep and imaging by Advertising Technologies, Inc., Atlanta, Georgia

Book design by Martha Gill and Vivian Mize

FOR CHARLEY & CAROLINE,

ENJOY

CONTENTS

Introduction *xi*

modern
Grill & Garden

LET'S PLAY OUTSIDE! – It is a tradition in my family to enjoy the outdoors fully. No, we aren't robust mountain-climbing types, but we do appreciate the seasons and all that comes with them. Having a family retreat has been a part of our collective past for longer than I can remember. In 1928, my father's father purchased a property on Steamboat Lake in Minnesota, close to the Canadian border, from one of his law partners, a Norwegian count who had built the property to remind him of his homeland. My grandfather,

I'M NOT THE ROBUST MOUNTAIN-CLIMBING TYPE. ARE YOU?

Roland J. Faricy, believed the northern wilderness would be the ideal summer refuge for his wife and their four boys while he continued to work back home in the city of St. Paul. ❀ This retreat consisted of 200 acres of shoreline and timberland and three cabins: the family cabin, a large lodge with a master bedroom and fireplace; the kitchen and dining cabin; and the boys' "sleeping" cabin. In those days, vegetables, milk and chickens were procured from a nearby farmer, and wild rice (cheaper than potatoes) was purchased from the Chippewa Indians. The boys caught walleyed pike and crayfish from the lake and picked cherries and wild berries from the nearby woods. My grandfather would arrive most summer weekends from St. Paul via the Great Northern railway. These weekends often began with the Steamboat Special. A drink unique to the lake, it was concocted with a jigger or two of bourbon, just-pumped well water, lake ice from the previous winter and a sprig of mint just picked from the kitchen garden. ✿ Many years have gone by, and the retreat is still in our family but a long way from our Georgia home. My father and mother decided to continue the family tradition of a refuge and purchased a villa over-looking a marsh on Amelia Island Plantation. Many of the photographs in this book were taken at this

WE'VE LEARNED TO MAKE THE MOST OF OUR COMPACT OUTDOOR AREA

secluded nature preserve on the east coast of northern Florida. While I spent my childhood summers at a Minnesota lake, my children are acquiring a different set of memories—of shell-filled shores, dunes and bonfires on the beach. But while we pack up and head for the coast whenever we can, we certainly can't spend entire summers there. Most weekends it's just not possible to load up for a six-hour drive from Atlanta. ✿ When we are not at the beach, we still want to enjoy ourselves outdoors in the best and easiest way possible. We have a small deck off our kitchen, and I have learned how to make the most of our compact outdoor area by gardening in containers, pots and other objects I've found. There is

little room for furniture, so I centered four beautifully crafted teak chairs around an ottoman, which serves as a table as well as a foot rest. For larger gatherings and cookouts, I have also added an everyday wooden picnic table, a few cast-off chairs and an old wicker rocker that needs a coat of spray paint every few years. This odd assortment has hosted just about every gathering in this book. ✿ Often these days when I am entertaining, I am asked just

ADD AN EVERYDAY
WOODEN PICNIC TABLE
FOR LARGER GATHERINGS

what is "modern"? Well, to me it includes a fun, relaxed attitude, whether cooking, decorating or

anything else. Modern is a way of living that doesn't take itself too seriously. It means pulling out your mother's ancient metal lawn furniture and using it with what you have or with a select new purchase. It means mixing together a mojito (a modern version of the Steamboat Special), firing up the grill and calling all your friends. Like me, you probably don't have the inclination to make homemade yogurt for a summer brunch—but how about adding freshly chopped mango or stirring instant coffee into your favorite vanilla brand? Instead of fussing over an elaborate flower arrangement, why not create a simple centerpiece of ornamental grass and flower blooms that lasts for months, or sow wildflowers at random in a bare patch of the garden? And don't forget, grilling means never having to cook alone! ✿ I

hope this fresh, contemporary approach to living well outside will inspire you to make

the most of your outdoor space, and help you turn it into your own retreat. I also hope you will

find that living a modern lifestyle is liberating. And that most of these outdoor living ideas are longer on style than

time. Whatever your space—an estate, a patio, a backyard or a balcony—it provides a chance to get out into the

open air and enjoy life. Entertaining outside can be very relaxed and informal. Dessert and accompaniments can

be made ahead of time. Invitations issued on short notice. And much of the cooking done while sipping your

beverage of choice in the beautiful outdoors. The most complex decisions you might face are charcoal, wood or

gas as fuel, and whether to use a covered or open

grill. It's up to you. Many avid grillers use primarily

DON'T RESTRICT
GRILLING AND GROWING
TO SPRING AND SUMMER

lump charcoal or wood as fuel and prefer to work on an open grill. They often divide the coals into sections,

creating low, medium and very hot areas of the grill. But charcoal- or wood-fueled grills can also be covered. A

covered grill is designed to be used with the lid in place and greatly speeds up cooking times; they are available in

charcoal or gas models. To be practical, the gas grill option is quicker, less messy and arguably the most modern

(meaning easy and fool-proof) way of creating a heat source. The majority of gas grills have low, medium and high settings that produce the same effect as varying coal temperatures.

In the chapters that follow you will also find *chef's notes* and other tips for outdoor cooking and seasonal dining. ❀ Each chapter of *Modern Grill & Garden* showcases a different outdoor gathering, with an appropriate garden theme and fare to laud the season. From an early winter barbeque to an autumn harvest to a twilight celebration of the first budding flowers and tastes of spring, you'll see that the fun of grilling and growing outside needn't be restricted to the summer months. ❀ The menus for *Modern Grill & Garden*, featuring every-thing from hot dogs and turkey burgers to hot

TURN TO YOUR HOME,
KITCHEN, GARDEN & PLANET
FOR REFRESHMENT

elderberry wine, roasted oysters and bento box picnic fare, were developed by Shaun Doty, the executive chef of the very modern Mumbo Jumbo Bar & Grill in Atlanta. Shaun's interest in grilling has also led him to Smith & Hawken, where he demonstrates updated grilling techniques and seasonal vegetable cookery. Walter Reeves, columnist, host of *The Georgia Gardener* on public television and horticultural educator at the University of Georgia, offers imaginative and practical ideas for each party that range from establishing a butterfly garden to showcasing winter berries to growing greens and lettuces in pots. Both Walter and Shaun bring a good measure of spontaneity and creativity to the gourmet gardener. Finally, an extensive Resource Guide listing Internet sites, food purveyors, gardening stores and catalogues and outdoor furnishing sources will help you turn

THE GOURMET GARDENER
LOVES TO RESIDE...OUTSIDE

inspiration into reality. ✿ Keep in mind as you read this book that it's not the definitive book about grilling, nor is it the definitive book about gardening. It is a guide to living well—outdoors. And as you turn to your home, kitchen, garden and planet for refreshment, I hope that you and your friends and family enjoy your retreat!

Martha Gill

Chill fresh juices in an ice-filled metal tub so guests can help themselves.
Include bottled water to keep everyone hydrated into the afternoon.

Morning Sun

BUTTERFLIES ARE FREE – What better metaphor for summertime than the butterfly? Beautiful, peaceful, polite, almost lazy—all in all, the perfect guest for a hazy summer brunch. Inviting butterflies is easy: just include plants in your garden that store nectar at the base of their flowers, such as butterfly bush, lantana and zinnias. Coaxing your human guests out of their cocoons calls for different enticements—chicken sausages with grilled pineapple, soft boiled eggs in vintage egg cups and silver dollar pancakes cooked in a cast-iron pan right on the grill. We designed the menu to be served whole or in parts. Follow your whim (and your appetite) and pick the dishes that reflect your morning mood. The simplest and lightest option: hot coffee, freshly squeezed fruit and vegetable juices, and a selection of yogurts and doughnuts from your favorite shop (we like Krispy Kreme). Remember, it's a summer weekend, and you deserve a bit of freedom after a week of captivity. The sun won't be around forever. Nor, alas, will the butterflies. But like many humans, these floating jewels become more active in the afternoon, as the day grows warmer. Another reason to linger over this liberating brunch.

MAKE A WISH ON THE
MORNING STAR

Planting for butterflies must take into account both the caterpillar and the butterfly stages of their lives. When a caterpillar breaks free of its tiny egg, it must have certain plants nearby to feed on or it will die. Likewise, when a butterfly emerges from its cocoon, the nectar of certain flowers must be provided or it will perish. That's why it's important to plant sources of food for caterpillars as well as for butterflies. Since there may be more than one generation of adults from spring through fall, you will need plants that bloom in each of these seasons. This also ensures that you have continuous flowers to enjoy. The accompanying lists give good choices.

All of the plants on both lists require a sunny garden spot. Begin by digging the soil to a depth of at least eight inches. Mix in two cubic feet of organic matter (compost, bagged cow manure, etc.) per each eight square feet of bed. Decide where to place each plant, taking into account their differing shapes. Some of the plants grow tall and columnar (fennel, milkweed), while others are short (parsley) and/or wide (butterfly bush). Check the label on each plant for its size when full-grown and space them accordingly. A simple design to attract swallowtail butterflies is to use a row of parsley in front; a mixed row of aster, money plant and coneflower behind the parsley; and a row of fennel and butterfly bush behind the smaller plants.

If you want to attract butterflies but have little room in your garden for additional plants, build a mud puddle for them. Fill a birdbath or clay saucer with wet soil or sand. Mix in a handful of rich topsoil, scoop a depression in the middle, then water as needed to keep it moist. A few slices of banana will provide the smell of rotting fruit that some butterflies love. Butterflies will visit the watering hole often to feed on the salts and protein dissolved in the mud.

Caterpillar Food

Milkweed – monarch
Queen Anne's Lace – swallowtail
Parsley – swallowtail
Marigold – sulfur
Snapdragon – buckeye
Fennel – swallowtail
Clover – sulfur
Passionflower vine – fritillary

Butterfly Food/Season of Bloom

Money plant – early
Lilac – early
Butterfly bush – mid
Butterfly weed – mid
Bee balm – mid
Purple coneflower – mid
Black-eyed Susan – mid
Aster – late
Petunia – continuous
Verbena – continuous
Lantana – continuous
Zinnia – continuous

FRESHLY SQUEEZED FRUIT AND VEGETABLE JUICES
SOFT BOILED EGGS IN EGG CUPS
SILVER DOLLAR WHOLE-WHEAT PANCAKES
SELECTION OF FLAVORED YOGURTS
GRILLED CHICKEN SAUSAGES AND PINEAPPLE
KRISPY KREME DOUGHNUTS

FRUIT AND VEGETABLE JUICES

Carrot Ginger Juice

- 20 carrots, washed but not peeled
- $1/2$ pound ginger, peeled

Following manufacturers instructions, combine ingredients and run through juice machine.

Beet and Pineapple Juice

- 1 pineapple, peeled, cored, and roughly diced
- 1 pound ruby red beets, peeled and diced

Following manufacturers instructions, combine ingredients and run through juice machine.

Tomato and Cilantro Juice

- 30 roma tomatoes, washed, quartered, and juiced with a juicer
- 1 bunch cilantro, chopped

In a stock pot over medium heat, cook tomato juice until reduced by half. Chill. When cold, add cilantro and salt and pepper to taste.

Each juice serves 8

 Please … don't make doughnuts from scratch! Head for the nearest drive-through when you wake up— who cares if you're driving in a robe?

SOFT BOILED EGGS IN EGG CUPS

• 8 fresh organic eggs

Gently lower eggs into a pot of boiling water. Cook for exactly 4 minutes. Remove from water with a slotted spoon. Tap one end of each egg with a spoon and peel away top. Serve in an egg cup with coarse salt.

Serves 8

SILVER DOLLAR WHOLE-WHEAT PANCAKES

Chef's note: Use a well-seasoned cast-iron skillet over a hot grill to make these pancakes.

• 2 cups whole-wheat flour
• 3 tablespoons baking powder
• 1 teaspoon salt
• 2 cups milk
• 4 eggs, separated
• 1/4 cup peanut oil, plus more for skillet

In a large mixing bowl sift together flour, baking powder, and salt. In a medium mixing bowl combine milk, egg yolks, and peanut oil. Add wet ingredients to dry. Whip egg whites until stiff and fold into batter. Lightly oil skillet and preheat over high heat or a hot grill. Using a ladle, drop batter onto skillet in 1-ounce portions. Cook pancakes until bubbles appear. Flip and cook on opposite sides until golden.

Serves 8

FLAVORED YOGURT

Chef's note: Vanilla makes an excellent base for these recipes. You can also experiment with yogurt from sheep and goat milk, available at many farmers markets. They are excellent combined with any of the flavors listed.

- 3 quarts vanilla yogurt
- 2 ripe papayas
- 6 tablespoons instant coffee
- 1 cup canned cranberry compote

Divide the yogurt among three bowls. Peel the papaya, remove the seeds, and cut into medium dice. Add the papaya to 1 quart of yogurt and stir to mix. Stir the instant coffee into another quart of the yogurt and the cranberry compote into the remaining quart.

Serves 8

GRILLED CHICKEN SAUSAGES AND PINEAPPLE

- 1 ripe pineapple, cored and peeled
- 3 pounds chicken sausage links
- 1/4 cup peanut oil

Prepare the grill. Slice the pineapple into 1/2-inch slices. Rub the pineapple slices and sausage links lightly with oil. Prick the sausages with a fork to prevent bursting on the grill. Place both on a hot grill. Cook the sausage, turning, until done, about 8 to 10 minutes. Grill the pineapple, turning, just until it is well scored with grill marks, about 4 to 5 minutes. Sprinkle with kosher salt and serve.

Serves 8

 Serve homemade yogurt out of mixing bowls, doughnuts out of the box. For a no-hassle tablecloth, try cheesecloth.

Revive vintage bedspreads as tablecloths and tea towels as placemats. Or stop by the fabric store and pick up swaths of fabric in floral and fruit prints. Never worry about hems; just bunch and tuck.

Garden Party

A SENTIMENTAL JOURNEY – Take a stroll into 1940s small-town America, stopping at the cute white bungalow on the corner for a garden party quite unlike the ones Aunt Marge used to host. Imagine a playful afternoon, a riot of peonies, red ripe cherries and old-fashioned placesettings. Here in your own backyard, a festive luncheon awaits you and your friends, with grilled and chilled pearl pasta salad, easy zucchini carpaccio and chicken pinwheels with luscious layers of Swiss chard, mozzarella and Parma ham. Harvest baby lettuce from your garden and toss together a salad with lemon thyme vinaigrette. To quench your thirst and elevate your spirit, stir up a light-hearted punch with a hint of effervescence. Then top it all off with sundaes made modern by caramel ice cream, chunks of biscotti and fresh cherries. Go with the decade and pull off some madcap hijinks. Play badminton and lawn croquet. Swing dance on the lawn to old Cab Calloway or Louis Jordan songs. Keep the punch flowing and the music hopping, and even the stuffiest guests might sneak off for a smooch behind the peony bushes.

SEARCHING FOR OUR GRANDMOTHER'S GARDEN

Our garden focus is on planting a variety of lettuce. Oak leaf and radicchio are especially easy to grow in containers. Peonies and other old-fashioned flowers make sweet centerpieces. If these aren't in your garden repertoire, we suggest ordering from the florist, or make a beeline to your local farmers market. Fix your eyes on peony blooms in full-bodied pinks and yellow-greens. Also select marigolds, daisies and zinnias for the look of just-picked garden bouquets.

Have you ever heard the expression "a mess of greens"? When you order a mesclun salad at a tony restaurant, that's all it is: a mixture of colorful greens and baby lettuces! You can grow your own mesclun mixture in a pot or window box.

To grow their best, greens and lettuce need plenty of sunshine, warm soil and cool air temperatures. You can buy started seedlings at your local nursery or you can start your own indoors. Fill a container three-fourths full with potting soil. Scatter seeds thinly on the soil and cover with another half-inch of soil. Water gently. Keep the pots in a warm spot until the seeds germinate. When the sprouts are an inch high, move to the sunniest window available. The pots can go outside when the danger of a hard freeze is past.

If you don't have room to farm inside, plant seed outdoors in early spring, when temperatures are likely to go below freezing only a few more times. Planting is simple: Scratch the tilled soil a bit, sprinkle seeds lightly and pat them into place with your hand. Water gently and you're through! Fertilize once when the plants are two inches tall and again when they pass four inches. Use any houseplant fertilizer, following the instructions on the label.

All of our lettuces and greens listed here grow well together and like the same conditions. Rather than growing only one kind of plant in a container or garden corner, try mixing the different seeds together, then planting, for a hodgepodge of color. After a few weeks you can harvest the biggest leaves with scissors. It's fun to give a couple of freshly washed leaves to guests for an impromptu taste test, then mix a salad to their order!

Lettuces

Red oak leaf—sweet "lettucey" taste, grows well in hot or cold conditions

Lollo rossa—frilly leaves, green at center, red on edges

Greens

Mizuna—deep green leaves, mild taste

Red mustard—use the leaves in a sandwich instead of searching for the Grey Poupon

Red Russian kale—blue-green leaves, stems turn reddish-purple if grown in cold weather

Arugula—add a peppery tang to the salad mixture

Baby spinach—thumb-sized, gray-green leaves provide mild flavor

Radicchio—wine-colored crunchy leaves grow in a head (like cabbage)

Sorrel—medium-green leaves, slight lemony tang

 This red oak leaf lettuce is ready for harvesting. Trim a bit here and there for your own organic salad.

MODERN PUNCH

BABY LETTUCE SALAD

GRILLED ZUCCHINI CARPACCIO

GRILLED CHICKEN ROULADE WITH SWISS CHARD,
MOZZARELLA AND PROSCIUTTO DI PARMA

GRILLED AND CHILLED PEARL PASTA SALAD

CARAMEL AND CHOCOLATE BISCOTTI SUNDAES

MODERN PUNCH

- 4 quarts ginger ale
- 1 (12 ounce) can mango or pineapple nectar
- 1 liter rum
- 1 pint lemon sorbet, softened

In a large punch bowl combine ginger ale, nectar, and rum. Float softened lemon sorbet on top.

Makes about 5 quarts

BABY LETTUCE SALAD

- 2 pounds assorted baby lettuces and greens, such as lollo rossa, oak leaf, arugula, sorrel, radicchio and baby spinach
- Juice of 3 lemons
- $1/4$ cup white balsamic vinegar
- 1 tablespoon thyme leaves
- $3/4$ cup extra-virgin olive oil

Gently rinse the lettuces and greens and spin dry. In a bowl combine the lemon juice, vinegar, and thyme leaves. Slowly whisk in the

Pressed glass, painted plaster molds and items such as this eye-catching pitcher are characteristic of the forties and fun to collect. Turn to the Resource Guide in the back of this book for some good places to start.

olive oil until vinaigrette is thick and emulsified. Add salt and pepper to taste. Just before serving, lightly dress the leaves with the vinaigrette. Finish with additional freshly ground black pepper.

Serves 8

GRILLED ZUCCHINI CARPACCIO

- 4 anchovy fillets, finely chopped
- 1 teaspoon finely chopped rosemary
- $1/2$ cup extra-virgin olive oil, divided
- 4 zucchini, very thinly sliced lengthwise
- 2 pints sunflower or radish sprouts
- Juice of 1 lemon
- 3 shallots, finely chopped

Prepare the grill. Combine anchovy, rosemary, and half the oil in a shallow baking dish. Dredge the zucchini slices in the seasoned oil and place flat on a baking sheet. Lightly season with salt and pepper. Grill on the hottest portion of the grill for 30 seconds per side, until just marked. Divide sprouts among 8 plates. Place slices of cooked zucchini on top. Drizzle with remaining olive oil and lemon juice and sprinkle with shallots. Serve at room temperature.

YOU MAY CATCH A GLIMPSE OF FLOPSY, OR EVEN PETER, IN YOUR LETTUCE GARDEN

Serves 8

GRILLED CHICKEN ROULADE WITH SWISS CHARD, MOZZARELLA AND PROSCIUTTO DI PARMA

- $1/2$ pound Swiss chard
- $1/4$ cup plus 1 tablespoon extra-virgin olive oil
- 3 pounds boneless skinless chicken breasts
- 2 cloves garlic, chopped
- 1 teaspoon dried oregano
- 4 ounces thinly sliced prosciutto di parma
- 8 ounces fresh mozzarella, grated

Prepare the grill and preheat the oven to 400°. In a large pan sauté Swiss chard in 1 tablespoon of the olive oil until wilted. Cover a cutting board with plastic wrap. Lay out the chicken cutlets so that they touch each other and form a square (8 x 8 inches). Cover with additional plastic wrap. With a meat mallet, pound cutlets until they are $1/4$-inch thick. Remove the top layer of plastic. Coat the chicken evenly with 2 tablespoons of the oil, the chopped garlic, and oregano. Arrange the prosciutto on top of the chicken. Top this with Swiss chard, then mozzarella. Season with salt and pepper. Roll the chicken carefully and bind securely with butcher's twine in 4 places. Using your hands, oil roulade thoroughly with remaining oil. Grill on medium heat until well browned, about 12 minutes. Transfer to a roasting pan and cook in oven for 25 minutes. (Alternatively, if your grill has an upper shelf, transfer the roulade to this shelf and close the lid to roast for 25 minutes.) Allow chicken roulade to rest on a cutting board for 10 minutes. Slice into 1-inch slices, discard string, and serve.

Serves 8

 Experiment with different types of pasta—orzo, couscous and pearl pasta each add a unique shape and personality to this side dish you can make ahead.

GRILLED AND CHILLED PEARL PASTA SALAD

- 1 (5 ounce) box pearl pasta*
- 1 large zucchini, halved lengthwise
- 3 red bell peppers, quartered and seeds and stems removed
- 4 portobello mushroom caps
- 1 large yellow onion, peeled and cut into $1/4$-inch slices
- $1/2$ cup peanut oil
- 1 cup grated Parmigiano-Reggiano
- $1/4$ cup peeled, seeded, and diced tomato
- 1 tablespoon chopped garlic
- 2 tablespoons chopped chives
- $1/4$ cup chicken broth
- $1/4$ cup extra-virgin olive oil

*see Resource Guide

Prepare the grill. Prepare the pasta according to package directions. Drain, place pasta in a bowl, cover, and chill. Brush the zucchini, bell peppers, mushroom caps, and onion slices lightly with vegetable oil. Grill vegetables until tender. Allow to cool. Cut into $1/8$-inch dice. In a large bowl combine the pasta with the grilled vegetables, cheese, tomato, garlic, and chives. Put chicken broth in a blender or food processor and, with the machine on high speed, slowly add the olive oil. Pour this mixture on top of the pasta. Mix, season with salt and pepper to taste, and chill.

Serves 8

spring luncheon

CARAMEL AND CHOCOLATE BISCOTTI SUNDAES

Chef's note: Use one or all of these toppings for delicious and nostalgic results.

Caramel Ice Cream

- 1 cup sugar, divided
- 2 $1/2$ cups half-and-half
- $1/2$ cup cream
- 8 egg yolks

Put half of the sugar in a large stainless steel saucepan. Heat over medium-high heat until the sugar begins to caramelize and turn golden brown. Add cream, half-and-half, and the remaining sugar and return mixture to a boil. This must be done quickly while stirring to prevent cream from boiling over. Remove from heat. Place the yolks in a large stainless steel bowl. Gradually ladle the hot cream into the yolks, whisking constantly, until the yolks are completely incorporated. Set the bowl on top of a pan of simmering water and cook, whisking constantly to prevent the eggs from curdling, until the mixture has slightly thickened. Remove from heat and place over a bowl of ice. Chill until cold. Freeze the mixture in an ice cream maker according to manufacturer's directions.

Makes 1 quart

Don't have enough sundae dishes for a crowd? Mix up different dishes—two generous scoops in each. Once they are filled with creamy ice cream and toppings you'll wonder why you ever thought you needed a matched set.

Chocolate Biscotti Crumbles

- $^1/_2$ pound chocolate biscotti

Chop biscotti into small pieces. Store in an airtight container until ready to use.

Whipped Cream

- $^1/_2$ cup cream
- 2 tablespoons powdered sugar

Beat the cream and sugar until cream is stiff.

Chocolate Sauce

- 4 ounces bittersweet chocolate, chopped
- $^1/_2$ cup heavy cream
- 1 ounce Kahlua

Combine all ingredients in a small saucepan and warm until the chocolate is melted. Reserve warm.

To Make Sundaes:

- 4 ripe bananas, sliced in $^1/_2$-inch pieces
- 8 fresh cherries
- 8 mint leaf sprigs
- 1 tablespoon powdered sugar

Place two scoops of caramel ice cream into each sundae glass. Top with bananas, biscotti, whipped cream, chocolate sauce, and fresh cherries. Add mint sprigs and dust with powdered sugar. Serve immediately.

Serves 8

spring luncheon

Update sun tea by using decaffeinated tea bags and adding orange citrus slices or vanilla bean (scrape out seeds and add to jar, pod and all). Allow to steep in the sun, pour over ice and enjoy.

Catching Rays

LOUNGE LIZARDS – Lounging poolside always seems to be modern, whatever the era. From a Roman villa to a Hollywood mansion, placid pool waters have reflected thousands of modern little gatherings over the ages. Why not add yours to the list? This early summer supper is just the place to start. The goal is a sophisticated meal so easy to prepare that you hardly need to get up from your chaise lounge. Recline as refreshing sun tea brews in clear jars and jugs. Serve simple tea sandwiches you've made earlier in the day. Grill lobster right in the shell. At the end of the day, you and your guests may rouse yourselves enough to make ice milk with an old-fashioned hand-cranked machine. Catching rays is about everything that is refreshing under the sun. In fact, the right amount of exposure to sunlight is vital to living a healthy, balanced life. Too much of a good thing, of course, is a problem. So find the best wide-brimmed hats, sunscreen and shade for protection. Stack cushions, covered in the latest (water-resistant!) fabrics, creating impromptu lounges and chairs. Learn about the ease of cultivating a water garden, then lay back and watch water lilies gently float in large, low ceramic containers. Whatever you do, don't hurry; with each idle, lazy minute, you'll be upholding a great tradition.

SUMMERTIME, SUMMERTIME, SWEET, SWEET SUMMERTIME

A pygmy water lily, duckweed and a terra-cotta pot are all that is needed to create this stunning poolside arrangement.

To create a water garden, start by choosing the container. Ideally you can find a waterproof ceramic pot to suit your fancy, but don't despair if your first choice has a drainage hole in the bottom. Simply cut a piece of plastic from the bottom of a used black plastic pot and seal it over the hole with a waterproof glue, such as Goop™. If your pot is terra-cotta, paint the inside with concrete sealer such as Drylock™, allow to dry, then rinse several times to remove any contaminants. A wooden half-barrel lined with a plastic liner makes a nice alternative for a more rustic look. Before buying any plants, make sure your container is watertight. Fill it with water. Don't tolerate even a pinhole leak.

In nature, some water-loving plants grow roots in the bottom muck and send their leaf-bearing stems to the water surface. Other plants eschew soil contact completely and float freely on top of the water. At a nursery that carries water garden plants, several large tubs will be filled with plants growing in submerged pots. Smaller tubs will contain various floating plants. Ask the nursery expert how large the plants will become. Suitably informed, you can choose plants that won't crowd your container.

Plants growing in pots might not have stems long enough to rise above the water surface of your container. Use an inverted clay pot or a couple of half-bricks underwater to provide a platform on which the submerged pot can rest. You'll get more water lily blooms if you fertilize the submerged-root plants with special nutrient tablets. Lilytabs™ are easy to insert into the soil and release their nutrients slowly.

Remember that, like you, almost all water plants are sun lovers!

Floating Plants

Water fern
Water hyacinth
Duckweed
Water lettuce

Submerged Root Plants

Pygmy water lily
Calla lily
Pickerel rush
Dwarf cattail
Dwarf papyrus

VANILLA AND CITRUS SUN TEAS

WATERCRESS TEA SANDWICHES

GRILLED LOBSTER IN THE SHELL

MARINATED CANTALOUPE WITH AGED GOUDA

VANILLA ICE MILK

WATERCRESS TEA SANDWICHES

Chef's note: As an accompaniment to the tea sandwiches, purchase freshly harvested French or another mild variety of radishes at your farmers market. Scrub clean, trim stems to 1 inch, and serve over ice.

- 2 cups packed watercress, washed and finely chopped
- 1 cup mayonnaise
- 1 loaf sliced pumpernickel bread, crusts removed
- 1 cup thinly sliced radishes

In a small bowl combine watercress, mayonnaise, and salt and pepper to taste and mix well. Spread the filling onto half the bread slices and top with remaining bread. Cut each sandwich diagonally to create 4 small sandwiches. Top each sandwich with 3 to 4 radish slices and serve.

Serves 6

 Add a terra-cotta pot to your outdoor serving pieces, fill with ice and use to keep drinks, fresh veggies and whatever else you can think of crisp and cool.

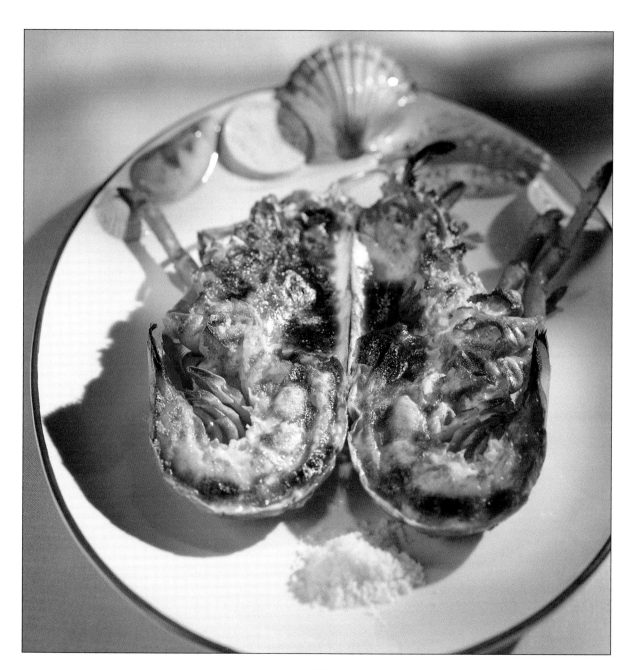

GRILLED LOBSTER IN THE SHELL

- 6 (2 pound) live Maine lobsters
- $^1/_2$ pound (2 sticks) butter
- $^1/_2$ cup Italian breadcrumbs
- 1 tablespoon chopped chives
- 1 teaspoon red chili flakes
- 3 lemons, halved

Bring a large pot of salted water to a rolling boil. Add whole lobsters, head first, to boiling water. Cook for 5 minutes. Remove and allow to cool to room temperature. Leave the head and body together and briefly rinse under cold water. Split lobsters in half lengthwise by placing the lobster with legs underneath on a cutting board and placing the knife where the tail meets the body. Cut, slicing through the head, then turn lobster and slice through the tail. Remove entrails from cavity. Prepare the grill and preheat the broiler. Put butter in a small saucepan and place on the grill until butter is melted. Brush each lobster with about 1 tablespoon of butter. Remove the saucepan from the grill and reserve the remaining butter. Season the lobsters with salt and pepper, and place them, flesh side down, on a medium-hot grill. Grill for 7 to 8 minutes, turn, and grill for 1 minute. Remove and transfer to a baking sheet. Combine breadcrumbs with half of the remaining butter, the chives, and the chili flakes. Mix well, then cover the lobster with the mixture. Place lobsters under broiler briefly to toast the breadcrumbs. Place a lemon half on each plate, crack the claws with the blunt edge of a chef's knife or nutcracker, and serve immediately.

Serves 6

In the mid-seventeenth century, a chef employed by Charles I of England developed a technique of shaking flavored cream into a dish of ice. This "ice milk" became so popular that the king kept the formula a "Royal Secret."

MARINATED CANTALOUPE WITH AGED GOUDA

Chef's note: Aged gouda is imported from Holland and has a dry, flinty texture and a toffee flavor that complements the melon.

- 1 cantaloupe
- $^1/_2$ cup late-harvest riesling
- 6 ounces aged gouda

Split cantaloupe and remove seeds. Cut into 6 wedges. Brush riesling over melon slices. Slice the aged gouda into the thinnest slices possible. Arrange over the melon slices and serve.

Serves 6

VANILLA ICE MILK

Chef's note: Ice milks contain less milk fat and solids than ice cream. The result is a lighter texture more like a sorbet than an ice cream. A hand-crank ice cream maker doesn't need an electrical outlet, so it's ideal for an outdoor gathering.

- 4 vanilla beans
- 1 quart milk
- 1 quart cream
- $^1/_2$ cup sugar
- 1 cup corn syrup

Split the vanilla beans lengthwise and scrape the seeds into a heavy-bottomed saucepan. Add the vanilla bean pods, milk, cream, and sugar. Heat to a simmer and simmer for 1 minute. Remove from heat and add the corn syrup, stirring until it is fully incorporated. Place the saucepan in a bowl of ice. Chill until cold and strain. Freeze the mixture in an ice-cream maker according to manufacturer's directions.

Makes 2 quarts

Eat your purple coleslaw! Vegetables are being bred these days to be more colorful and nutritious.

Backyard Cookout

LET'S TWIST AGAIN – It's been done and done and done—so why not do it again? But this time with a twist—a modern one. The backyard cookout is one of those things in life that never grows old, because it can be forever interpreted and updated without losing its original charm. It's simple to turn your own all-American backyard into picnic-table chic.

The look is retro, but with necessary updates—like garden incense instead of bug bombs, kitchen hand towels for napkins and big, floppy Gerber daisies. We all know that a cookout is a great way to entertain a large group, and serving buffet-style is always less trouble. But the very best thing about a cookout is how easy it is to put everyone to work. Send volunteers to the grocery store to pick up root beer and last-minute fixings.

EVERYTHING YOU NEED IS IN YOUR OWN BACKYARD

Charge one or two barbecue experts—there are a few in every crowd—with manning the grill. Have domestic types mix and form the turkey burgers. Kids can help set out ready-made relishes, paper plates and plastic utensils. The host's real work will have been done the day before: mixing up versions of two cookout classics, potato salad and cabbage slaw, and creating a fresh and seasonal strawberry rhubarb trifle. Our garden choice for this gathering, centerpieces of bright flowers and grasses, is fresh, simple and original. Arrange the grass around the outer edge of a decorative pot (we choose classic terra-cotta) and nestle two or three flowers inside. Now kick back, relax and enjoy the great outdoors.

Flowers

Cosmos

Dutch iris

Gerber daisy

Poppy

Shasta daisy

Snapdragon

Sweet William

Zinnia

Grass seed and alternatives

Annual rye

Perennial rye

Fescue

Alfalfa seed—Guests can snip it from the pot to garnish their salads.

Mondo grass—Buy it from a nursery ready-grown and arrange in your pot. Mondo grass is a perennial evergreen, hardy outdoors from Kentucky southward.

For outdoor table settings, a combination of new grass and "planted" flowers is more appropriate than a bouquet of hothouse flowers.

It's easy to grow grass (though frustrated lawn lovers may beg to differ!). Three weeks before your planned soiree, fill a decorative clay pot three-quarters full with potting soil. Sprinkle a table-spoonful of grass seeds on top, then cover with a thin layer of soil. Gently moisten the soil and slide the pot into a clear plastic food storage bag. Set the pot on a sunny windowsill.

Within ten days, the soil will be covered with the fine green hairs of newly sprouted grass. Remove the plastic bag and feed the grass with houseplant fertilizer. In another ten days the grass will be lush—ready to be given a "mowing" with kitchen scissors.

Now for the flowers! On the morning of the get-together, snip the freshest blooms from your garden or buy daisies or other bright flowers from your farmers market. Store them in the refrigerator in a plastic bag. Just before guests arrive, use a pencil to poke several holes in the center of the grassy centerpiece, cut the flower stems to an appropriate length and insert the flowers. The brilliant blooms of poppy, Gerber daisy, Sweet William, snapdragon or Dutch iris make a lush combination with emerald green grass.

Next day, remove the faded flowers and store the mini-lawn in a shady spot where it won't freeze. The grass should last for weeks if given an occasional watering and "mowing." Add fresh flowers for your next get-together.

Opposite: a vivid Gerber daisy encircled by mondo grass.

A & W Root Beer and Assorted Micro Brews

Turkey Burgers and Hotdogs

Mango Catsup and Muscadine Mustard*

Potato Salad with Creamy Tofu Dressing

Purple Slaw with Cinnamon and Orange

Strawberry Rhubarb Trifle

see Resource Guide

TURKEY BURGERS

- 6 pounds ground turkey
- 2 tablespoons chopped garlic
- $1/2$ cup chopped parsley
- 1 tablespoon chopped rosemary
- 1 green bell pepper, seeded and finely chopped
- 1 tablespoon black pepper
- 4 tablespoons salt

Prepare the grill. Mix all ingredients in a large mixing bowl. Form meat into 16 patties (about 6 ounces each). Grill patties, turning once or twice, until juice runs clear when pierced with a fork, about 4 minutes per side.

HOTDOGS

- 2 packages hotdogs (8 per pack)

When the hamburgers are finished, place the hotdogs on the grill. Cook for 4 to 5 minutes, turning often.

Serves 12 to 16

 Don't happen to have vintage Fiestaware on hand? Go for the Chinette®. It's as sturdy as ever, and recyclable.

POTATO SALAD WITH CREAMY TOFU DRESSING

- 3 pounds Russet potatoes, scrubbed
- 2 cups soft tofu
- $1/3$ cup Dijon mustard
- 1 cup chicken broth
- 3 shallots, peeled
- $1/2$ cup vegetable oil
- $1/3$ cup finely diced celery
- $1/3$ cup chopped chives

Cook the whole potatoes in boiling water until tender. Drain and let cool. Peel the potatoes and slice into $1/4$-inch slices. Place in a large bowl. In a blender or food processor combine tofu, mustard, chicken broth, and shallots. Puree until smooth. With the machine running, add the oil in a steady stream until the dressing is thick and emulsified. Pour dressing over potatoes. Add celery, chives, and salt and pepper to taste. Serve chilled.

Serves 12

PURPLE SLAW WITH CINNAMON AND ORANGE

- 1 large head red cabbage, thinly sliced
- 5 orange segments, halved
- Juice and zest from 1 orange
- 1 tablespoon ground cinnamon
- $^1/_3$ cup sugar
- $^1/_2$ cup peanut oil
- 1 tablespoon salt

Combine all the above ingredients, adding more salt to taste. Allow to marinate, chilled, at least 3 hours. Toss before serving.

Serves 12

STRAWBERRY RHUBARB TRIFLE

Cake
- 1 cup sugar
- 8 eggs
- 2$^1/_2$ cups flour, sifted

Preheat oven to 350°. Butter and flour two 8-inch cake pans. With an electric mixer, beat eggs and sugar until mixture has increased by $^1/_3$ in volume. Add flour in three batches, making sure it is thoroughly incorporated before adding the next batch. Pour the batter into the cake pans, spreading it toward the sides so the centers are slightly concave. Tap pans gently to remove any air bubbles. Place on top rack of oven and bake for 25 minutes. Allow the cakes to cool in the pans for 1 hour. Remove from the pans and completely cool.

Burn incense sticks which come in a package like the one pictured above, in your garden during a cookout. The smoke keeps away pesky flying insects and smells infinitely better than bug bombs.

Pastry Cream

- 1 vanilla bean
- 1 cup sugar
- 5 egg yolks
- $^{1}/_{2}$ cup flour, sifted
- 2 cups milk
- 1 tablespoon chilled butter
- 5 gelatin sheets

Split vanilla bean lengthwise and scrape out seeds into a large mixing bowl. Add sugar and egg yolks to the bowl. With an electric mixer, beat until mixture is very light in color. Add flour and mix just to combine. In a large saucepan bring the milk to a boil. Pour over egg mixture, whisking, and pour mixture back into saucepan. Return to heat. Cook, whisking constantly, until the mixture has considerably thickened. Remove from heat and add butter. Soak gelatin sheets in cold water until softened. Remove gelatin from water, add to warm pastry cream, and stir to combine. Reserve this mixture in a warm area so gelatin will not set.

Rhubarb Compote

- 1 pound rhubarb, peeled and chopped into 1-inch pieces
- 1 cup sugar
- 1 cup water
- $^{1}/_{4}$ cup grenadine

Combine all ingredients except grenadine in a saucepan and bring to a boil. Simmer until mixture has reduced and thickened to a jam-like consistency. Add grenadine, remove from heat, and reserve at room temperature.

Whipped Cream

- 1 cup cream
- 4 tablespoons powdered sugar

Whisk cream and sugar together until cream is stiff. Chill.

Simple Syrup

- $1/4$ cup sugar
- $1/4$ cup water

Combine sugar and water in a small saucepan and boil until sugar dissolves. Remove from heat and reserve at room temperature.

To Assemble Trifle:

- Cakes
- 1 ounce Grand Marnier
- Simple Syrup
- Rhubarb Compote
- Pastry Cream
- 2 pints strawberries, washed, hulled, and halved
- Whipped cream

Using a serrated knife, slice the cakes horizontally into 2 layers each. Place 1 layer in a 3-quart trifle bowl, trimming away the excess. Combine the Grand Marnier with the Simple Syrup and brush over the cake. Spread $1/4$ of the Rhubarb Compote on top, followed by $1/4$ of the Pastry Cream. Distribute $1/4$ of the strawberries evenly over the cream. Repeat with the remaining 3 layers of cake, brushing each with the Grand Marnier and Simple Syrup mixture and topping with Rhubarb Compote and Pastry Cream. To finish, use a pastry bag to pipe whipped cream decoratively on top. Allow to chill at least 4 hours before serving.

Use trivets and leaves for table decoration. The plastic plate on top of the ceramic pie plate "charger" (metal pie tins work too) is part of a camp set from the seventies, found at a bargain basement thrift store. Vary your place settings. Mix it all up, use what you have or get it cheap.

Autumn Harvest

A CHILL IN THE AIR — When you see the first autumn leaf tumble down from the sky, invite a few good friends to celebrate the harvest season. Create a barnyard setting with birdhouses, pansies and sunflowers. Plant a kitchen garden that will flourish in cooler weather, filled with ornamental kale, red cabbage and rosemary. Fill a basket or two with sugar maple leaves to complete the rural look. Plan a trip to the flea market or look around your basement and garage for "found objects" such as wooden crates and tin cans for planting—even an old sink can have a second life as a plant container for ornamental kale and cabbage. Recycle bottles and jars as vases for fall flowers. Do as much or as little as you wish to set this natural mood. Falling leaves and the brisk air alone will be enough. Have fun with a menu designed to make the most of current trends toward fresh produce, organic farming and locally produced foods. Seek out and support your local artisanal bakeries, consummate butchers, small-scale organic farmers and other passionate purveyors of high-quality, low-quantity foods. These culinary pioneers are making entertaining easier for us all. Enjoy a glass of a full-bodied red wine while the duck marinates in honey and olive oil. Learn to grill unconventional choices, such as fruits and baby squash for risotto. Add a whimsical touch and set out honey "bears" for clover honey parfaits. After your efforts, take time to relish this party—autumn, after all, is the season for reflection.

FIND AND SUPPORT YOUR LOCAL ORGANIC FARMERS BY VISITING OFTEN

Look for frilly leaves when selecting ornamental cabbage. This pair of ornamental cabbages are cozy companions to the common pansy when snugly planted in a weathered tin.

ORNAMENTAL KITCHEN GARDEN

Something exciting is occurring in the autumn outdoor garden: Common vegetables have begun to be used as ornamentals. Red-stemmed chard, deep-green parsley, frilly-leafed kale and deep-purple cabbage provide texture and color in the cool season landscape. They can be used alongside pansies in all but the coldest part of the country to make exciting combinations in the autumn garden.

Check with your local nursery to find which cool-season vegetables are appropriate for your area. Cool-season plants, whether vegetables or pansies, require very soft soil in which to grow. If your garden soil is the least bit hard to dig, mix compost or composted manure deeply into the earth. If you can easily force your index finger entirely into the soil, it is soft enough to make a good home for your plants.

Gently pull your plants from their pots and lay them on their sides in the spots where you plan to plant them. How do the colors combine? Is there too much white from the ornamental cabbage on one side of the bed? Do the crinkled parsley leaves look too busy beside the frilly kale? Did you buy enough pansy plants to place them no more than six inches apart from each other?

When the whole bed is planted, use liquid houseplant fertilizer (diluted according to directions) to give the plants their first feeding. Keep the fertilizer handy: The plants need to be fed every three weeks for as long as they last. Those with limited space can take heart: The ornamental vegetables listed combine exceedingly well with pansies in containers. They can be grown outdoors for a few weeks, then brought inside for table centerpieces.

Cool-Season Plants

Red cabbage

Parsley

Rosemary

Ornamental kale

Pansy

Chives

Swiss chard, especially "Bright Lights"

Ornamental cabbage

Lettuce

BEAUJOLAIS NOUVEAU

ESCAROLE SALAD
WITH RED ONION AND ORANGE VINAIGRETTE

GRILLED DUCK BREAST
WITH VERJUS SAUCE AND GREEN GARLIC SPROUTS

SQUASH BLOSSOM RISOTTO WITH GRILLED BABY SQUASH

CLOVER HONEY PARFAITS WITH GRILLED FRUITS

ESCAROLE SALAD WITH RED ONION AND ORANGE VINAIGRETTE

- 2 cups freshly squeezed orange juice
- $1/2$ cup extra-virgin olive oil
- 2 cups champagne vinegar
- $1/2$ cup sugar
- 2 red onions, peeled, cut in half, and thinly sliced
- 2 heads escarole, washed, dried, and roughly chopped
- $1/2$ cup orange segments

In a medium saucepan simmer the orange juice until it is reduced to $1/4$ cup. Place in a blender or food processor. With the machine running, slowly drizzle in the olive oil until it is fully incorporated and reserve. In a saucepan boil vinegar with sugar until the sugar is dissolved and pour over sliced onions. Allow to cool. Place the escarole in a large bowl and toss with the orange vinaigrette. Transfer to 6 individual serving plates. Remove onion slices from vinegar and divide over salads. Garnish with orange segments and serve at once.

Serves 6

Ask your local coffeehouse for extra burlap coffee bags and cloth sugar bags, like the one pictured under the platter opposite. They make great outdoor table covers and placemats.

47

GRILLED DUCK BREAST

Chef's note: Garlic sprouts can be found in many farmers markets during the spring and fall. This recipe also calls for verjus, a traditional condiment made from the juice of unripe grapes pressed before the harvest. In French, verjus means green juice.

- 1 (6 pound) duck breast, split, fat and connective tissue removed
- $^1/_2$ cup extra-virgin olive oil
- $^1/_4$ cup honey
- $^1/_4$ cup sugar
- 1 tablespoon butter
- 2 cups verjus*
- 1 cup veal sauce or demi-glace*
- 36 green garlic sprouts or green onions, trimmed
- Peanut oil

* available in gourmet food shops or see Resource Guide

The night before: Place the duck breast halves in a shallow dish. Combine the olive oil and honey and pour over the duck. Marinate in the refrigerator overnight.

Place the sugar in a large saucepan. Cook over high heat until sugar begins to turn golden and caramelize. Add butter. When melted, add the verjus, being careful not to splatter. Continue cooking over high heat until liquid is reduced to a syrupy consistency. Add the veal sauce and return to a boil. Simmer for 1 minute. Skim any fat off the top and season with salt and pepper to taste. Reserve in a warm place. Prepare the grill. Remove duck from the marinade, season with salt and pepper, and place on the grill, skin side down. Avoid the hottest part of the grill. Cook the breast for 10 minutes, until it is well crisped. Turn and cook for 2 to 3 minutes. At the same time, lightly brush the garlic sprouts or green onions with peanut oil and place them on the grill, avoiding the hottest part.

Widely used in medieval and Renaissance times, verjus is making a comeback. Use on salads, in sauces and for seasoning foods. The sour taste heightens flavors and is similar to vinegar or lemon juice.

Remove the breast and sprouts. Allow the duck to rest for 2 minutes. Slice the breast on a diagonal and arrange the slices on a warm platter. Top with 10 to 12 sprouts and the sauce, add salt and pepper, and serve immediately, with additional sprouts on the side.

Serves 6

SQUASH BLOSSOM RISOTTO WITH GRILLED BABY SQUASH

- 2 cups whole baby squash, such as yellow squash or patty pan
- $1/4$ cup extra-virgin olive oil
- 1 garlic clove, minced
- 1 shallot, minced
- 2 tablespoons chilled butter, divided
- 2 cups arborio rice
- 6 cups hot chicken broth
- 1 cup squash blossoms, cleaned
- $1/2$ cup grated Parmigiano-Reggiano
- $1/4$ cup chopped Italian parsley

Prepare the grill. Toss squash in oil and grill over high heat, turning, for 5 minutes, or until cooked. Reserve warm. In a large stockpot sauté the garlic and shallots in 1 tablespoon of butter for 1 minute. Add rice and stir to coat with butter. Add $1/3$ of the broth and stir with a wooden spoon until it is nearly absorbed. Add $1/3$ more of the broth and continue to cook, stirring, until nearly dry. Add the final $1/3$ of the broth, stirring until the rice is the consistency of a thick soup. This should take about 20 to 25 minutes. Add the squash blossoms and cook 3 minutes more. Remove from heat and allow to sit for 1 minute. Add remaining butter and cheese and stir to combine. Adjust seasoning and divide among 6 plates. Top with grilled squash and parsley.

Serves 6

CLOVER HONEY PARFAITS WITH GRILLED FRUITS

- 2 cups cream
- 1 cup sugar
- 4 egg yolks
- 3 tablespoons clover honey
- 1 ounce Grand Marnier
- 1 vanilla bean, split
- 2 each ripe peaches, nectarines, and mangoes
- 2 tablespoons peanut oil
- 6 mint leaves
- $^1/_4$ cup powdered sugar

Whip cream until it is stiff. Refrigerate. In a mixing bowl combine the sugar, egg yolks, honey, Grand Marnier, and vanilla bean. Set the bowl over a saucepan of simmering water and whisk the mixture until it has doubled in volume and is very light in color. Remove from heat and continue whisking over a bowl of ice until the mixture has cooled to room temperature. Remove vanilla bean. Fold in reserved whipped cream and transfer to a 2-quart mold. Cover and freeze overnight.

Prepare the grill. Slice the peaches and nectarines into 8 wedges each. Peel the mangos and slice into $^1/_4$-inch wedges. Toss the fruits in peanut oil. Grill fruit slices just until they are soft and slightly marked. Remove and keep warm. Briefly immerse the parfait mold in a warm water bath, run a knife around the edges, and invert it onto a cutting board. Divide fruit among 6 plates. Dip a knife into warm water and slice parfait into even portions. Garnish with fresh mint leaves and powdered sugar.

Serves 6

 Set out 1 or 2 honey bears to drizzle extra honey over the parfaits and grilled fruits. These little creatures are available at supermarkets everywhere.

You can purchase spouts separately at many kitchenware shops. The spouts fit nicely into oil and vinegar cruets or empty wine bottles.

Herbal Roast

A WINTER'S TALE — The trees are bare, save for clusters of dried berries and an errant, clinging leaf or two. It's too early for snow, too early for the holidays. And yet, it is winter, and you long for the glow of a wood fire and the cozy warmth that comes from looking out a frosted window at a barren world. Now is the perfect time for an early winter gathering. Depending on where you live and the whims of the weather, this get-together for a crowd can work inside or out—or maybe a bit of each. Even if you find yourself manning the grill alone in the cold, you may be surprised at how invigorated you'll feel bundled up before the glowing coals. (Then again, you may be cursing silently as your hands turn a dangerous shade of white and you lose all sensation in your toes.) Your guests, meanwhile, will be warm as toast, sipping hot elderberry wine in front of a roaring fire. Winter is no time to give up the garden. Many shrubs and trees, such as holly, nandina, crabapple and hawthorn, berry in the winter. Prune carefully and use the branches to decorate a room. If you happen to be a city dweller, go to your favorite farmers market, garden shop or florist and bring home holly, pyracantha, boxwood or magnolia leaf branches. In keeping with the increased energy and appetites of this season, we've created a menu that's a showstopper. The star is a pork rib roast prepared with a Memphis rub, served with grilled root vegetables. We provide easy recipes for making your own flavored oils for the vegetables. And for dessert, caramel lady apples add a touch of nostalgia at this most nostalgic time of the year. But because we're all grown up now, we present the apples with Italian panettone, a sweet yeast bread studded with raisins, citron, pine nuts and anise. Just slice and serve. On this evening, as you look up at the clear night sky, you might be reminded that there are things in life we all love. One is to gather.

WINTER'S FIRST FROST AND CHILL CAN BE WELCOMING... WHEN A WARM FIRE AWAITS

The thorny rugosa rose is so hardy it actually can survive almost as far north as the Arctic Circle.

WINTER BERRIES

There are almost as many berry colors as there are hues of flowers. Yellow, orange, purple, white and scarlet berries adorn bushes and small trees. Hidden in fall by foliage, winter berries come into their own in the colder months, when they are highlighted against the stark bare branches of a winter landscape. They cry out to be used in outdoor and indoor displays.

To have winter berries in your garden, plant shrubs and trees that are renowned for their ornamental fruit. Small crabapples, such as the varieties "Callaway" and "Donald Wyman," bear iridescent scarlet fruit. The red berry clusters of nandina and some hollies make great holiday decorations. If your planting area is small, search out dwarf forms of berry-producing plants, such as Purple Beautyberry (*Callicarpa dichotoma*). Though bare stems covered with berries are beautiful in their own right, oftentimes evergreen foliage makes a good backdrop for some compositions. You may already have several evergreen broadleafed shrubs, such as holly and nandina, in your landscape. In the northern half of the country, most evergreens have needles instead of leaves. A combination of small branches of blue spruce, fir and winterberry holly is stunning!

Some plants on our lists may not be hardy in every corner of the country. Check with your local nursery for variety recommendations for your region.

Plants with Colorful Berries:

Holly

Beautyberry

Viburnum

Nandina

Toyon (California holly)

Crabapple

Pyracantha

Aucuba

Mahonia

Rugosa rose

Hawthorn

Plants with Evergreen Leaves:

Holly

Osmanthus

English laurel

Magnolia

Autumn fern

Mahonia

Camellia

Gardenia

Loropetalum

Nandina

Photinia

Aucuba

Carolina cherry laurel

Pittosporum

Boxwood

ELDERBERRY WINE

RADICCHIO SALAD WITH PRESERVED LEMON
AND GREEN GODDESS DRESSING

PORK RIB ROAST WITH MEMPHIS RUB

ROOT VEGETABLES WITH FLAVORED OILS

CARAMEL LADY APPLES WITH PANETTONE

RADICCHIO SALAD WITH PRESERVED LEMON AND GREEN GODDESS DRESSING

- 1 preserved lemon*
- 3 heads radicchio, cored
- $1/4$ cup cream
- $1/2$ cup mayonnaise
- 2 ripe avocados, peeled, pitted, and cut into bite-sized pieces
- Juice of 3 lemons
- 1 tablespoon chopped parsley
- 1 teaspoon cayenne pepper

available in gourmet food shops or see Resource Guide

Quarter preserved lemon. Remove and discard flesh and pith. Cut peel into julienne strips the size of match sticks and soak in cold water. Tear radicchio leaves into bite-sized pieces and place in a large bowl. In a food processor combine cream, mayonnaise, avocados, lemon juice, parsley, and cayenne. Process until smooth. Add salt to taste. Drizzle the dressing over the radicchio, toss, and garnish with lemon strips.

Serves 8

Soak fresh herbs and place over fire or coals for outdoor aromatherapy.

PORK RIB ROAST WITH MEMPHIS RUB

Chef's note: The brining process removes excess blood and strong flavors. This Memphis rub recipe is inspired by the dry spice rubs typically used in Tennessee barbecue joints. To add even more flavor to this rib roast soak wood chips overnight and use as fuel. The size of the wood chips you use depends on the size of your grill, using large chips for large grills and smaller chips for small grills.

- 2 quarts water
- 3 cups kosher salt
- 1 pork rib rack (chine bone removed) with 8 large chops
- $^1/_4$ cup peanut oil
- 1 (8 ounce) can unsalted beef broth
- $^1/_2$ cup honey
- 20 sage leaves, chopped

Memphis Rub
- 4 tablespoons paprika
- 1 tablespoon cumin
- 1 tablespoon garlic powder
- 4 tablespoons brown sugar
- 1 tablespoon black pepper
- 1 tablespoon cayenne pepper

The day before: Combine water and kosher salt in a large bowl and add the pork roast, adding more water if necessary to completely cover. Place in refrigerator and let sit overnight. Remove the roast from brine, discarding liquid, and pat dry. Combine the Memphis rub ingredients and coat the surface of the roast thoroughly. Using your hands, cover the roast with the peanut oil. Preheat the oven to 400° and prepare the grill. Grill pork roast, turning, until the meat is well colored on the outside. This should take at least 10 minutes. Transfer the roast to a roasting pan and place in the oven. Roast the meat until an instant-read meat thermometer registers 150°, about

20 minutes. Remove from oven and allow to rest while preparing sauce. In a small saucepan combine broth and honey and cook over high heat until mixture is reduced by half. Add sage and salt to taste. Slice the roast between each chop. Serve sauce separately.

Serves 8

ROOT VEGETABLES WITH FLAVORED OILS

- $1/2$ pound each small baby rutabaga (2 to 3 inches), choggia or ruby red beets, sweet potatoes, and turnips
- 4 bay leaves
- 1 teaspoon black peppercorns
- $1/4$ cup vegetable oil, divided
- Salt and freshly ground black pepper
- Flavored Oils (recipes follow)

Preheat oven to 400°. Scrub vegetables under cold running water. Combine all vegetables in a roasting pan. Add 1 inch of water, bay leaves, peppercorns, half of oil, and salt. Cover with foil and roast for 1 hour, or until vegetables are tender. Remove vegetables from liquid, discarding liquid, and allow to cool. Prepare the grill. Using a small knife, peel each of the vegetables, being careful to leave them whole. Place in a large bowl. Mix with remaining oil. Season with salt and freshly ground pepper to taste. Grill the vegetables just until grill marks appear and the vegetables are heated through. Serve with your choice of flavored oils.

LIGHT YOUR WINTER GARDEN WITH TIKI TORCHES

Serves 8

Chef's note: These oils are not designed to cook with but are used as condiments, to add flavor to cooked foods. The rosemary oil and Thai chili oil have a 2 week shelf life. The paprika oil will last about 1 month.

Rosemary Oil

- 2 cups extra-virgin olive oil
- 1 large sprig of rosemary
- $^{1}/_{4}$ cup black peppercorns

Place all of the ingredients in a saucepan. Over medium heat, heat until bubbles begin to appear. Remove from heat and allow oil to cool. Carefully transfer the contents of the saucepan to a glass bottle or jar. Allow this to infuse overnight. Seal to preserve flavor.

Thai Chili Oil

- 2 cups peanut oil
- 20 whole Thai chili peppers

Gently crush peppers with the underside of a sauté pan or the flat surface of a large knife and transfer to a saucepan. Cover with oil and slowly heat until peppers are simmering. Remove from heat and allow oil to cool. Carefully transfer the oil and peppers to a glass bottle or jar. Infuse overnight. Seal to preserve flavor.

Paprika Oil

- 2 cups peanut oil
- $^{1}/_{2}$ cup paprika

Place paprika into a glass bottle or jar. Add oil and shake vigorously to combine. Allow the ingredients to infuse for 2 days. After this time the paprika will have settled to the bottom of the jar. Use as is or decant oil into another jar, leaving behind sediment.

Flavored oils can be used with a wide variety of foods. Enjoy drizzled over pasta, salads, or vegetables.

CARAMEL LADY APPLES WITH PANETTONE

Chef's note: Panettone, a leavened yeast bread with raisins and candied fruits, is a traditional Italian holiday treat. In the recipe below it is served along with caramel lady apples. Lady apples are small, sweet apples. Suitable substitutes are jonagold or McIntosh.

- 8 lady apples or other small, sweet apples
- 8 wooden popsicle sticks
- $1/2$ cup chopped pecans
- 2 cups prepared caramel apple mix
- 1 panettone, sliced*

* available at gourmet food shops or see Resource Guide

Wash and dry the apples. Insert a stick into the top of each apple. Place the pecans in a shallow dish. Warm caramel according to package directions. Dip bottom half of apples into caramel, then roll in the pecans. Place apples on waxed paper and allow to set. Serve with panettone slices.

Serves 8

A plywood board supported by level stones makes a low table; layer table runners for a covering. Regular bed pillows with cotton cases are cozy seating. Toss sand and branches right on the "table." Everything will come out in the wash.

Seaside Grill

Close your eyes and think of the sea. Imagine a shell-filled beach with white sand dunes and sea grass rustling in the breeze. A bonfire lights the scene. The sun is dropping from the sky, a perfect sphere sinking into the sea. The table is set with translucent linens, woven hemp runners and shells plucked from the beach. Best of all, it's time to eat. To stir the palate, serve your guests chilled manzanilla, the straw-colored, bone-dry Spanish sherry that carries a hint of the sea. Nibble on black mission figs wrapped with Parma ham and a warm dandelion salad. Then savor grilled salmon from the sea. We serve it with

TEN YEARS SEARCHING IN THE DEEP FOREST, TODAY GREAT LAUGHTER AT THE SEA

caper-raisin sauce. Of course, we all can't pack up and go to the beach for the weekend. (Some of us really do live in Kansas.) But you can turn this seaside fantasy into reality easily enough by having plenty of shells and driftwood around and leading your guests through some impromptu Zen rock gardening with these beach artifacts. After the "gardening" and the meal, close with dessert. Start by learning some Italian: "panna cotta" means "cooked cream." It's a light, silky egg custard, worthy of silent contemplation on a star-filled night—no matter how far you are from the sea.

Zen, a centuries-old philosophical and religious belief system, emphasizes meditation and contemplation of the problems, truths and joys one encounters on the path to enlightenment. In today's world, Zen has come to take on a much looser and more general meaning, encompassing all sorts of profound thinking and meditations. As your guests arrive, invite them to seek enlightenment by creating their own Zen gardens.

Zen teachers instruct their students how to assemble stones, small plants, sand and, perhaps, flowing water to make a small site suitable for personal introspection. So instead of building sand castles at the beach, gather traditional karesansui (dry gardening) items such as sand, stones, shells and driftwood, then create your own Zen garden by the sea. Use fork tines or a small whisk broom to make ripples and waves around rocks and shells. Spoons can flatten the sand around a particularly smooth stone. Allow the tide to ebb and flow around your designs. Later in the evening, in the reflections of the fire, share reflections on life in these modern times.

Seven Principles of Zen Gardening

Simplicity—uncrowded
Tranquility—an oasis of calm
Ordinariness—using found natural materials
Spaciousness—lead the eye from spot to spot
Spontaneity—playful, effortless
Asymmetry—no formal arrangement
Incompleteness—things could yet happen

CHILLED MANZANILLA

FIGS WRAPPED IN PROSCIUTTO

WARM DANDELION SALAD WITH
BACON AND SOURDOUGH CROUTONS

GRILLED RED PEPPERS WITH
SWEET MARJORAM AND GORGONZOLA

GRILLED SALMON WITH CAPER-RAISIN SAUCE

PANNA COTTA WITH VANILLA

FIGS WRAPPED IN PROSCIUTTO

- 1 pound imported thinly sliced prosciutto
- 12 ripe black mission figs, halved

To serve, arrange the slices of ham on 6 plates. On each plate place 4 fig halves on top of the prosciutto.

Serves 6

WARM DANDELION SALAD WITH BACON AND SOURDOUGH CROUTONS

- 2 cups cubed sourdough bread
- 2 tablespoons extra-virgin olive oil
- Pinch of salt
- 1 pound young, tender dandelion leaves
- $1/2$ cup diced cooked bacon (about 20 slices)
- $1/4$ cup sherry vinegar
- 6 hard-boiled eggs, thinly sliced

Preheat the oven to 300°. Combine bread and oil in an ovenproof pan. Toss with salt. Toast in the oven, stirring frequently, for approximately 10 minutes, or until crispy.

 For true beachside gatherings, make sure candle flames are protected by glass lanterns. It's nearly impossible to keep an open candle lit at the beach. And pack a good flashlight... just in case.

Wash and dry the dandelion leaves and transfer them to a large mixing bowl. Add croutons. Cook bacon in a small saucepan over medium heat until crispy. Immediately pour fat and crisped bacon over the dandelion leaves. Return the pan to the heat, add the vinegar and bring to a boil. Pour over the salad evenly and quickly, season with salt and pepper, and toss. Arrange the salad on individual serving plates and garnish with egg slices.

Serves 6

Grilled Red Peppers with Sweet Marjoram and Gorgonzola

- ¹/₂ cup balsamic vinegar
- 12 red bell peppers
- ¹/₂ cup extra-virgin olive oil, divided
- ¹/₂ cup crumbled Gorgonzola
- ¹/₄ cup marjoram leaves

Prepare the grill. In a small saucepan boil balsamic vinegar until reduced by half. Toss the whole bell peppers in 2 tablespoons oil. Grill on the hot portion of the grill until skin is blackened and peppers have deflated. Allow the peppers to cool, pull each pepper in half, and remove the skin, stems, and seeds. Arrange peppers on a serving platter and drizzle with remaining oil and reduced balsamic vinegar. Season with salt and pepper and top with cheese and marjoram leaves.

Serves 6

Chef's note: When cooking over an open pit or with wood, keep a cup of water nearby to flick over the flames. This helps to control the cooking and avoid flare-ups.

- 6 (6 ounce) salmon fillets
- 1 teaspoon red pepper flakes
- 1 tablespoon finely chopped rosemary
- $1/4$ cup extra-virgin olive oil

Caper-Raisin Sauce

- $1/4$ cup golden raisins
- 2 cups sherry vinegar
- $1/4$ cup capers, drained

Prepare the grill. Place the salmon in a large shallow dish. Combine the red pepper flakes, rosemary, and olive oil and pour over the salmon. Allow to marinate in the refrigerator for at least 30 minutes and up to 24 hours. Combine raisins and vinegar in a bowl and allow raisins to soak 3 to 4 hours until softened. Place raisins, vinegar, and capers in a blender or food processor. Puree until smooth. The consistency should be thick but pourable. Remove the fish from the marinade and season with salt. Place the salmon fillets on the hottest potion of the grill and cook just until marks appear, about 1 to 2 minutes. Turn and cook just until marks appear. Move salmon to a medium-heat area of the grill and continue to cook, turning, until the fish flakes with a fork, about 6 to 8 minutes. Transfer to a serving platter and serve the caper-raisin sauce on the side.

Serves 6

 Lightweight trivets made of straw suit the seaside and outdoors better than traditional metal versions.

- 3 gelatin sheets
- 1 1/2 cups heavy cream
- 1/2 cup milk
- 1/4 cup sugar, divided
- 2 vanilla beans

Soften the gelatin in cold water. Combine the cream, milk, and 1 tablespoon of the sugar in a saucepan. Split the vanilla beans and gently scrape the seeds and pods into the mixture. Bring to a boil, and, stirring with a wooden spoon, simmer for 3 to 4 minutes. Remove from the heat and whisk in the remaining sugar and the gelatin until the gelatin is dissolved. Line a fine-mesh strainer with several layers of cheesecloth and strain the mixture into a large bowl, discarding vanilla pods. Place the bowl over a larger bowl of iced water and chill until mixture is cool to the touch, but do not allow it to set. Stir, then pour into 6 (3 ounce) ramekins. Refrigerate for at least 4 hours before serving. Immerse the ramekins in a bowl of hot water to loosen the panna cotta, then invert the ramekins onto 6 individual serving plates.

Serves 6

Twilight
Celebration

BLOSSOM BY BLOSSOM – The transformation of a bulb into a flower, winter to spring, a grit of sand into a pearl—each is cause enough to celebrate. Early spring, with its captivating hints at a warmer, lusher world just ahead, is the perfect time to bring your grill back to the center of the garden. And twilight is a beautiful time to be outside. But before you start cooking, start planting. Our garden focus tells you how to plant bulbs in the late fall in order to enjoy flowering plants for spring gatherings. Schedule your party two to three weeks after stalks and foliage appear. When the day arrives, you'll have shocks of color dotting the garden and delighting your guests.

A LITTLE MADNESS
IN THE SPRING —
IT'S A GOOD THING

Sophisticated dishes such as oysters and flatbreads are actually quite simple when prepared on a grill. When done properly, grilling oysters helps the shells open up neatly and easily, without resorting to power tools or cutting your hands to ribbons. Arrange the oysters and flatbreads on a large tray for a striking presentation. For cocktails, offer contemporary mojitos with fresh crushed mint leaves, and for dinner serve a lightly chilled white wine with floral notes, such as a riesling. As dusk arrives, bring out sweet pralines and light golden candles. Enjoy the gentle radiance of your early spring garden, and all the enchantment of twilight.

Just as internal temperature determines the success or failure of grilled food, soil and air temperatures determine most aspects of a bulb's life. You can forecast when you will have plenty of tulip, daffodil and hyacinth blooms if you notice when daily temperatures begin to average 50°F or above. Flowers start appearing three weeks later. Most spring-blooming bulbs must endure several weeks of chilly temperatures before they can send up a flower stalk. And the temperature in which bulb foliage grows after the blossoms have faded governs whether the plant will bloom once again next spring.

Planting bulbs in a landscape bed is simplicity itself. Begin in late fall, typically October and November for most parts of the country. Use a bulb-planting tool to make a hole six inches deep, drop in a bulb and cover it with the original soil you removed. Move to the next spot and repeat until tired and ready for hot cocoa. Rather than segregating different bulbs in different parts of your flower bed, create a riot of informal color by casting the mixed bulbs over the bed en masse and planting each one where it comes to rest. Is it too shocking for a purple hyacinth to nestle beside an orange daffodil and be overshadowed by a scarlet tulip? That's for you and Mother Nature to decide!

Spring-flowering bulbs announce the demise of winter.
Gather tulips in a gardener's trug to bring the cheer of spring indoors.

Alternatively, you can plant bulbs in containers and then "force" them to bloom much earlier than they would in nature by bringing them indoors after twelve weeks. Bulbs adapt easily to growth in containers, allowing you to use them as centerpieces and decorative accents inside or for outdoor gatherings. Plant the bulbs in clay pots or other containers, such as wooden crates, filled with potting soil. After watering thoroughly, place the pots in a discrete corner of your landscape and cover with a big pile of leaves. Twelve weeks later, dig through the pile and check your buried treasures. You should find the light green tips of bulb foliage peeking above the soil surface.

Having been chilled appropriately, your bulbs can be left in the pile until three weeks before you need them. Bring the pots indoors to a cool but well-lit spot. In just a few days the foliage will turn deep green and begin to grow tall over the pot rims. A week later the bloom stalks will emerge and begin to elongate. Seven days afterward, luscious blooms will begin to open.

MOJITO COCKTAIL

GRILLED OYSTERS WITH HERB BUTTER

CHILLED LEEK SALAD WITH BLACK TRUFFLE VINAIGRETTE

GRILLED FLATBREADS

PRALINES*

see Resource Guide

MOJITO COCKTAIL

- Juice of 1/2 lime
- 1 teaspoon sugar
- 2 ounces rum
- Splash of club soda
- Fresh mint leaves

Pour lime juice into a highball glass and add sugar. Fill glass with crushed ice. Add rum and club soda. Garnish with mint and muddle to crush.

Serves 1

GRILLED OYSTERS WITH HERB BUTTER

- 3/4 pound (3 sticks) butter
- 72 cold water oysters (see caption), scrubbed clean, 6 per guest
- 1/2 cup chopped parsley
- 1/2 cup chopped tarragon
- 1/2 cup chopped chives
- Juice of 8 lemons

Prepare the grill. Put the butter into a small saucepan and place it on the grill to melt. Reserve in a warm place. Arrange the oysters on

 Select oysters from cold water regions such as Washington state, Maine and Massachusetts.
Even in the spring, the northern water is so cold that these oysters are still in their winter season.

the grill in batches. Cook until they just begin to open, about 3 to 5 minutes. To shuck, hold an oyster in a towel. With your other hand, use an oyster knife to pry it open. Line a platter with kosher salt and arrange the oysters on top. Add the herbs to the warm butter. Season with salt and pepper. Spoon a little herb butter onto each oyster. Squeeze lemon juice on top.

Serves 12

CHILLED LEEK SALAD WITH BLACK TRUFFLE VINAIGRETTE

- 24 leeks, washed, outer layers removed, 3 inches of green only
- $^1/_2$ cup black truffle vinegar*
- $^1/_4$ cup chicken broth
- $^1/_2$ cup grapeseed oil
- $^1/_4$ cup peeled, seeded, and diced tomatoes
- $^1/_4$ cup chopped chives
- $^1/_4$ cup chopped shallots
- 2 pints alfalfa or sunflower sprouts
- 2 cups sourdough croutons (see page 68)

* available in gourmet food shops or see Resource Guide

Bring a pot of salted water to a boil, add the leeks, and boil for 8 minutes. Drain, rinse in cold water, and chill until needed. In a small airtight container with a lid, combine vinegar, chicken broth, and oil. Cover and reserve at room temperature. To serve, divide the leeks among 12 plates. Add salt and pepper to taste to the reserved vinaigrette. Add the tomatoes, chives, and shallots to the vinaigrette. Spoon over the leeks. Garnish with fresh sprouts and croutons.

Serves 12

To Make the Flatbread:

- 3 packets dry yeast
- 1 teaspoon sugar
- 3 cups warm water
- 11 cups flour
- 1 tablespoon salt
- $1/4$ cup extra-virgin olive oil

In a bowl mix yeast, sugar, and water and let stand for 20 minutes. Sift $9^{1}/_{2}$ cups of the flour into a large mixing bowl. Reserve additional flour for kneading and rolling out the dough. Add yeast mixture, salt, and olive oil to the flour and mix thoroughly by hand until you have formed a ball. On a lightly floured surface knead dough for 5 minutes until dough is pliable and elastic. Place the dough in a bowl large enough to contain it when it rises. Cover with a wet towel, place the bowl in a warm (not hot) place, and allow the dough to double in size. Divide the dough into 6 equal-sized balls. Roll out each ball into an 8-inch round. Stack the flatbreads, putting a sheet of wax paper in between each to prevent sticking. Chill the dough for 2 hours.

Arugula Pesto with Goat Cheese

- 1 cup garlic cloves, peeled
- $1/2$ cup extra-virgin olive oil, divided
- $1/2$ cup packed blanched arugula
- $1/4$ cup peanut oil for oiling the grill
- 1 cup fresh goat cheese
- 3 prepared flatbreads

 As twilight disappears, light lanterns and candles to continue the glow well into the night.

Sauté the garlic cloves in 3 tablespoons of the olive oil until they are soft and lightly browned, about 12 minutes. Keep warm. In a blender combine the arugula and remaining olive oil and puree until smooth. Season the pesto with salt and pepper to taste. Prepare the grill. With a dish towel, lightly oil the grill. Grill flatbreads, turning once, until they are well marked, about 3 minutes. Turn again and brush with a layer of pesto. Follow with small dollops of goat cheese and roasted garlic cloves. Close the cover of the grill to finish cooking for 1 minute.

Makes 3 flatbreads

Tomato, Zucchini, and Yellow Squash with Parmigiano-Reggiano

- $^1/_4$ cup peanut oil for oiling the grill
- $^1/_4$ cup extra-virgin olive oil
- 2 zucchini, thinly sliced crosswise
- 2 yellow squash, thinly sliced crosswise
- 5 roma tomatoes, thinly sliced crosswise
- 3 prepared flatbreads
- 3 tablespoons finely chopped rosemary leaves
- 1 cup grated Parmigiano-Reggiano

Prepare the grill. Using a dish towel, lightly oil the grill. Brush the zucchini, squash, and tomatoes with olive oil and put them on the grill to soften for 2 minutes. Place flatbreads on the grill and cook, turning once, until they are well marked, about 3 minutes. Turn the flatbread again and top with the grilled vegetables. Sprinkle with rosemary, cheese, and salt and pepper to taste. Close the cover of the grill to finish cooking for 1 minute.

Makes 3 flatbreads

Use petite cordial or liqueur glasses for offering your guests Calvados, Galliano, and sweet ruby port after dinner.

Moonrise Watch

YIN AND YANG – When was the last time you watched the moonrise? The ancient Chinese watched the position of the moon in the night skies to predict their fortune, and used the art of feng shui to improve their luck and create a sense of well-being. The philosophy of feng shui is simplicity itself—to enhance the quality of life by living in harmony with the forces of nature. You don't have to be a feng shui master to marvel at the order of the universe—or to predict a moonrise. When scheduling your party, just consult a Farmer's Almanac or the Astronomical Applications Department of the U.S. Naval Observatory (listed in the Resource Guide) for moonrise dates and times. Then position yourself perfectly by preparing

DANCE BY THE LIGHT OF THE MOON

for this sleek and sophisticated evening, influenced by Eastern style. Strike your own balance with a buffet of simple yakitoris. (In Japanese, yakitori means grilled, and refers to small pieces of marinated meats and vegetables threaded onto a skewer.) Create a tranquil mood with a succulent garden. Aside from bringing you good fortune, these desert plants are easy to care for and endlessly fascinating. As the moon brightens and the sky darkens, clear an area for cigar aficionados and serve a trio of after-dinner drinks. Offer Galliano, Calvados and a young, sweet ruby port. Sip, savor and thank your lucky stars as the celebration for moonrise unfolds.

Scratched by a barrel cactus? Break off a piece of aloe vera for natural relief.

SUCCULENT GARDEN

The Latin root of succulent is *succus*, meaning "juice." In arid regions, or where rain may be absent for months at a time, plants have evolved the ability to store water in their fleshy stems or leaves. Cacti are the most commonly known succulent plants, but there are thousands of others. Succulents require watering only once per month. They rarely need fertilizing. What could be more carefree?

Most ornamental succulent plants are not hardy outdoors where winter temperatures dip below freezing. They can be grown in a sunny, draft-free window during the cold months. When night temperatures are consistently above fifty-five degrees, succulents can be moved outdoors for the summer. Don't place them in full sunshine for at least a month. It takes that long for their skin to become accustomed to the strong rays of the sun. In fact, to avoid sunscald completely, your succulents can grow quite happily in light shade, out of direct sunshine.

Any container with a drain hole can be home to a succulent. Look for plain glazed ceramic pots or trough garden containers, made from light-weight concrete. Fill the container with a special soil mix made for cacti and their kin. Buy three or four small cactus specimens, remove them from their pots and place them in your container. To avoid injury, wrap a belt made from a thrice-folded paper towel around the body of the cactus, allowing both ends of the towel to extend beyond the body on both sides. Pinch the towel ends tightly, close to the cactus. Hold the towel ends to move the cactus. For an amusing accent, embed a fist-sized smooth stone halfway in the soil and top with a toy plastic lizard.

Easy-care Succulents

Aloe vera—long, thick, light green fingers taper to a point

Jade plant—thick leaves and stems make a dark green mound

Kalanchoe—often grown for its bright red flowers

Burro's tail—thread-like stems covered with fleshy stubs hang from a pot

Barrel cactus—short, stout and covered with spines

Sedum—several varieties, some standing upright, some lying prostrate

Bunny-ears cactus—yellow-green color; don't touch the soft-appearing spines

YAKITORI ASSORTMENT

CHICKEN DRUMETTES WITH THAI PEANUT SAUCE

AFTER-DINNER DRINKS — CALVADOS, GALLIANO, RUBY PORT

YAKITORI ASSORTMENT

Chef's note: Yakitoris are Japanese street food, always grilled and seared on skewers in the open air. If you use wooden skewers instead of metal, soak in water for 1 to 2 hours before grilling.

Flank Steak with Ginger and Cilantro

- $1/4$ cup chopped garlic
- $1/2$ pound ginger, peeled, half minced, half julienned
- 1 cup soy sauce
- 1 cup peanut oil
- 1 (2 pound) flank steak
- 20 bamboo skewers
- $1/4$ cup chopped cilantro
- Juice of 4 limes

In a large bowl mix the garlic, the minced ginger, soy sauce, and peanut oil. Add the flank steak to the bowl, making sure it is completely covered in the marinade. Marinate for a minimum of 2 hours in the refrigerator. Remove from the marinade and scrape away the excess seasoning and liquid. Prepare the grill. Place meat on the hottest portion of the grill, and cook for about 4 minutes per side for medium-rare to medium meat. Remove from heat and chill until cold. Remove steak from the refrigerator and, with a sharp knife, slice across the grain into 20 thin slices. Thread each slice onto a bamboo skewer. Top with the julienned ginger and chopped cilantro. Transfer to a platter and chill until ready to serve. Just before serving, squeeze the fresh lime juice over the meat.

Makes 20 yakitoris

 Modern design pioneers envisioned a world in which good design was used everyday and was within reach of everyone. This affordable fly swatter designed by Philippe Starck continues this modernist aesthetic.

Pork and Round Leek Barbecue

- 1 cup kosher salt
- 2 quarts water
- 4 pounds pork tenderloin (about 4 to 5 tenderloin)
- 12 leeks, washed, tops removed, and cut into $^1/_2$-inch rounds
- 20 bamboo skewers
- Peanut oil for grilling
- 1 cup prepared barbeque sauce

The night before: Dissolve the salt in the water. Immerse the pork loins in the brine and refrigerate. The next day, remove the pork and pat dry. Cut pork into cubes, prepare the grill, and preheat the broiler. Alternately thread pork cubes and leek rounds onto skewers. You should have about 4 pieces of leek and pork per skewer. Using a rag or towel, rub the oil carefully over the grill. Place the skewers on the grill and cook, turning, until pork is fully cooked, about 8 to 10 minutes. Remove the skewers and transfer to a baking dish. Cover with the barbecue sauce. Broil until the barbecue is well set and glazed on the pork. Serve immediately.

Makes 20 yakitoris

Marinated Jerk Swordfish

- 3 pounds swordfish, cut into 1-inch cubes
- 2 tablespoons prepared jerk seasoning
- 20 bamboo skewers
- Peanut oil for grilling

Prepare the grill. Sprinkle the swordfish cubes with salt and dredge them in the jerk seasoning. Thread the swordfish cubes onto skewers. Using a rag or towel, rub the oil carefully over the grill. Place the swordfish on grill and cook, turning, for 5 to 6 minutes until firm and cooked through. Remove promptly and serve.

Makes 20 yakitoris

Tofu and Mushrooms with Hoisin Glaze

- 3 pounds hard tofu, cut into 1-inch dice
- 80 cremini mushroom caps
- 20 skewers
- $1/2$ cup peanut oil
- 1 cup hoisin sauce

Prepare the grill. Assemble skewers, alternating tofu and mushrooms, about 3 cubes of tofu and 4 mushrooms per skewer. With a brush coat tofu and mushrooms with oil. Season with salt and pepper. Grill on a medium-high grill until well marked and mushrooms are cooked, about 8 minutes. Brush with hoisin sauce to glaze and transfer to a serving platter. Serve warm.

Makes 20 yakitoris

According to many feng shui masters, two cacti placed on either side of a front door are thought to ward off evil spirits and prevent loss.

Chicken Drumettes with Thai Peanut Sauce

- 40 chicken drumettes
- $^1/_3$ cup peanut oil
- 2 cups smooth peanut butter
- $^1/_2$ cup simple syrup (see page 41)
- $^1/_4$ cup fish sauce
- $^1/_4$ cup Thai sanbal sauce
- 1 cup chopped peanuts

Prepare the grill and preheat the broiler. Lightly rub chicken with salt and $^1/_3$ cup oil. Place on the grill and cook, turning, until the drumettes are cooked through and golden, about 10 minutes. Promptly remove from heat. In a medium bowl combine the peanut butter, simple syrup, fish sauce, and Thai sauce. Mix well. Brush the wings generously with the mixture and transfer to an oven-safe dish. Sprinkle chopped peanuts over the chicken and broil, watching closely, until peanuts are toasted.

Makes 40 drumettes

AFTER-DINNER DRINKS

Calvados – an apple fruit brandy

Galliano – an herbal, spicy vanilla liqueur

Ruby Port – a young, sweet port

spring evening buffet

Celebrate your own Woodstock for two.

Midnight Tryst

PEACE, LOVE AND UNDERSTANDING – It's still the Age of Aquarius, and some say love will steer the stars. Find out for yourself if it's true, and set out on a stargazing modern-day tailgate for two. Pack a basket with star charts and maps of constellations, and a telescope if you have one. Search for rolling hills, wildflowers and an open meadow for an epic view of the sky. A few supplies are essential. First, a cooler with a bottle of fine champagne on ice. Second (and almost as important), some good organic insect repellent. Third, a blanket large enough for two. A flashlight is optional, depending on your adeptness in the dark. Add a portable hibachi to put the finishing touch on the escabèche shrimp. Then prepare a bento box, a sectioned wooden box used in Japan during train travel for the ultimate in transportable food. Into the separate sections, tuck in pickled cabbage, fresh soybeans, Asian sesame noodle salad and black rice pudding. All can be made or purchased the day before. Take along a packet of wildflowers and sow as you go.

WE'VE GOT TO GET OURSELVES BACK TO THE GARDEN

WILDFLOWER GARDEN

Though the word "wildflower" might imply "carefree," a bit of forethought before planting will reward you with a spot that requires only minimal maintenance through the growing season. Your first choice is which seed mixture to buy. In the warmer parts of the country, a wildflower mix will include more annual plants (they can reseed themselves, given a long growing season). A mix for northern climes will have fewer annuals but more cold-hardy perennial plant seeds. You don't need to mix your own—your local nursery will likely have a seed mixture appropriate for your climate.

Common Wildflowers

Cosmos
Coreopsis
Cornflower
Black-eyed Susan
Butterfly weed
Corn poppy
Ox-eye daisy
Yarrow
Blanket flower
Lupine
Blazing star
Purple coneflower

Wildflowers can't compete with already-established grass or weeds. It's best to simply eliminate all plants in your native nook by spraying them with a weed killer that doesn't harm the soil or future plants. RoundUp™ and Finale™ are labeled for clearing away unwanted plants, and the chemicals disappear in a few days.

In most parts of the country, late fall planting is best. Scratch the bare soil a bit with a rake and sprinkle your seeds whither you will. Come spring, the annuals will sprout and provide you with months of ever-changing blossoms. Meantime, the perennial flowers will slowly establish themselves for the long term.

Caring for your plot is a two-part process. First, if grassy weeds begin to show their sprouts, pull them out before they spread throughout your patch. Second, do pick your flowers regularly. Trimming off the bloom stimulates a plant to produce more. If you fail to remove flowers each week, the wildflower season will be short. Each fall, use clippers or your lawn mower to shorten all plants to two inches tall. Though some plants will still have blooms, the clipping will improve the natural process of reseeding which occurs each winter.

Plan your bento box picnic in the summer, during the height of wildflower season.

FINE CHAMPAGNE

ESCABÈCHE GRILLED SHRIMP

ASIAN SESAME NOODLE SALAD

EDAMAME (COOKED SOYBEANS)

KIMCHEE (PICKLED CABBAGE)

FORBIDDEN BLACK RICE PUDDING

ESCABÈCHE GRILLED SHRIMP

Chef's note: As soon as you reach your destination, light the hibachi. You'll have a nice fire while you sip champagne. Once the fire has died and only hot coals remain, the time is right to grill the shrimp.

- 1 tablespoon sugar
- 3 tablespoons rice wine vinegar
- 1 tablespoon chopped cilantro
- 1 tablespoon chopped garlic
- $1/2$ red onion, peeled and julienned
- 12 large shrimp, peeled and deveined
- 3 tablespoons peanut oil

Prepare a hibachi. In a bowl combine the sugar, rice wine vinegar, cilantro, garlic, and onion. Brush the shrimp with peanut oil and grill until they are pink and no longer translucent. Transfer to the marinade and mix, coating the shrimp. Serve immediately, using a portion of the marinade as sauce.

Serves 2

 Pick up a star guide at a book store—as you and your companion gaze up at the stars together, recall Dom Pérignon's first words to his fellow monks upon tasting champagne for the first time: "Come quickly, I'm drinking stars!"

ASIAN SESAME NOODLE SALAD

Chef's note: Always be sure to drain noodles well after cooking so the dressing is not thinned. Never pat noodles dry; they tend to become soggy.

- 1 (8 ounce) packet of frozen Chinese egg noodles
- 2 tablespoons tahini paste
- $1/4$ cup cream
- 1 tablespoon fish sauce
- 1 tablespoon soy sauce
- $1/2$ tablespoon black sesame seeds
- $1/2$ tablespoon white sesame seeds

Blanch the egg noodles for 1 minute in a pot of boiling water. Immediately drain and refresh with cold water. Drain well. Combine them in a bowl with the tahini paste, cream, fish sauce, and soy sauce. Mix well. Garnish with sesame seeds.

Serves 2

FORBIDDEN BLACK RICE PUDDING

- 4 cups water
- 1 cup black rice*
- 1 cup milk
- 1 teaspoon vanilla extract
- 1 cinnamon stick
- Zest of $1^1/_2$ oranges, minced
- Zest of $1^1/_2$ lemons, minced
- 1 teaspoon minced ginger
- $^1/_2$ cup packed light brown sugar
- $^1/_2$ teaspoon salt
- 7 gelatin sheets
- 2 egg whites
- $^3/_4$ cup cream
- 1 ounce Grand Marnier
- 1 (6 ounce) can sweetened coconut milk
- 6 mint leaves

*available in Asian markets and some supermarkets,
or see Resource Guide*

Bring the water to a boil and add the black rice. Simmer the rice, covered, until it is al dente, about 25 minutes. Drain. In a stainless steel saucepan combine the milk, vanilla extract, cinnamon stick, fruit zests, ginger, brown sugar, and salt. Add rice and cook until the milk has reduced by half. Keep warm. Soak the gelatin in cold water for 2 to 3 minutes until softened. Add gelatin to the saucepan and stir to combine. Cool the mixture to room temperature. Beat the egg whites until they start to stiffen. Beat the cream until stiff. Add the Grand Marnier to the rice mixture, then fold in the beaten egg whites and whipped cream. Transfer to 6 (5 ounce) molds and

 A nearly empty champagne bottle makes a perfect vase for a wildflower.

chill for 4 hours. To unmold, dip the molds into hot water and then invert, shaking forcefully. Garnish with mint leaves. Serve with the sweet coconut milk as a sauce.

Serves 6

To Assemble Bento Box:

Chef's note: When preparing a bento box made of wood or lacquer, put the food in small ceramic bowls, then place the bowls in the bento box compartments. If you want to put the foods directly into the compartments, use plastic bento boxes instead.

- 4 ounces soy sauce
- 1 (6 ounce) jar of kimchee (pickled cabbage)*
- 1 (8 ounce) package of edamame (cooked soybeans)*
- Escabéche Grilled Shrimp
- Asian Sesame Noodle Salad
- 2 servings Forbidden Black Rice Pudding
- 2 bento boxes**

* available in Asian markets and some supermarkets
** see Resource Guide

Pour soy sauce into 2 bowls and transfer each to a compartment in each bento box. Divide the remaining dishes among the remaining compartments of the bento boxes.

RESOURCES

A.L. Bazzini
339 Greenwich Street
New York, NY 10013
212/334-1280
(dried fruits, nuts, chocolates)

Ad Hoc Softwares
410 West Broadway
New York, NY 10012
212/925-2652
(garden accessories, houseware, tableware)

Antique Addiction
436 West Broadway
New York, NY 10012
212/925-6342
(vintage tableware)

Anthropologie
375 West Broadway
New York, NY 10012
212/343-7070
215/564-2313 (for additional store locations)
(garden accessories, clothing, tableware)

Aphrodisia
264 Bleeker Street
New York, NY 10014
212/989-6440
(dried herbs)

Astronomical Applications Department
U.S. Naval Observatory
3450 Massachusetts Avenue NW
Washington, D.C. 20392
202/762-1617
http://aa.usno.navy.mil/AA
(sun and moon rise and set times)

Bella Cucina Artful Food
800/580-5674 (for catalogue)
(pearl pasta, gourmet foods)

Bridge Kitchenware
214 East 52 Street
New York, NY 10022
212/838-6746 (for catalogue)
(kitchenware)

Broadway Panhandler
477 Broome Street
New York, NY 10022
212/966-3434
(kitchenware)

Burpee Seed Company
300 Park Avenue
Warminster, PA 18991
800/283-5159 (for catalogue)
(bulbs, plants, seeds)

Callaway Gardens
The Country Store
800/280-7524
(muscadine mustard)

Calvin Klein Home
800/294-7978 (for nearest retailer)
(tableware)

Calyx & Corolla
800/800-7788
www.calyxandcorolla.com
(direct mail flowers)

Circa
www.circa50.com
(1950s tableware, ceramics)

Crate & Barrel
800/323-5461 (for catalogue and store locations)
www.crateandbarrel.com
(garden accessories and furniture, tableware)

Dean & Deluca
560 Broadway
New York, NY 10012
800/221-7714 (for catalogue)
www.dean-deluca.com
(black truffle oil, panettone, verjus, gourmet foods)

DOM (USA), Inc.
693 Fifth Avenue
New York, NY 10012
212/334-5580
(houseware, kitchenware)

Felissimo
10 West 56th Street
New York, NY 10019
212/247-5656
www.felissimo.com
(Asian tableware, bento boxes, star charts)

Ferrara

195 Grand Street

New York, NY 10013

800/533-6910

www.ferraracafe.com

(panettone, biscotti, pastries)

Fillamento

2185 Fillmore Street

San Francisco, CA 94115

415/931-6304

(garden accessories and furniture, tableware)

French Wyres

PO Box 131655

Tyler, TX 75713

903/597-8322 (for catalogue)

(garden furniture, plant stands, trellises)

Garden.Com

www.garden.com

(bulbs, plants, seeds, garden accessories and furniture)

Gardener's Eden

800/822-9600 (for catalogue)

(bulbs, plants, garden accessories and furniture)

Good Goods

http://www.goodgoods.tm.fr

(Philippe Starck's catalogue of non-products)

Gumbo Ya-Ya

219 Bourbon Street

New Orleans, LA 70130

504/522-7484

(pralines and spices)

Hancock Fabrics

601/842-2834 (for store locations)

www.fabric1.com

(fabrics, sewing accessories)

Holt's Cigar Company

2270 Townsend Road

Philadelphia, PA 19154

800/523-1641

www.holts.com

(fine cigars)

Home Depot

800/553-3199 (for store locations)

www.homedepot.com

(gardening supplies, ergonomic tools, plants)

Internet Antique Shop
800/294-2433 (for catalogue)
www.tias.com
(antiques, collectibles)

Lady Bird Johnson Wildflower Center
4801 La Crosse Avenue
Austin, TX 78739
512/292-4100
www.wildflower.org
(wildflower information)

Lemon Grass
367 West Broadway
New York, NY 10013
212/343-0900
(candles)

Lilypons Water Gardens
800/723-7667(for catalogue)
(water gardening supplies and plants)

Maruwa Supermarket
1737 Post Street
San Francisco, CA 94115
www.maruwa.com
415/563-1901
(black rice, Japanese foods supermarket)

Metropolitan Deluxe
1034 Highland Avenue
Atlanta, GA 30306
404/892-9337
(garden accessories, tableware)

The MOMA Design Store
44 West 53rd Street
New York, NY 10019
212/767-1050
800/447-MOMA (for catalogue)
www.moma.org/stores.html
(houseware, tableware)

Mood Indigo
181 Prince Street
New York, NY 10012
212/254-1176
(vintage tableware)

Moss
146 Greene Street
New York, NY 10012
212/226-2190
(20th-century industrial design products)

The National Bird Feeding Society

PO Box 23

Northbrook, IL 60065

847/272-0135

(backyard bird-feeding information)

New World Foods

20855 NE 16th Avenue, Suite 36

Miami, FL 33179

800/655-3665

(mango ketchup, grilling sauces)

Open Air Markets

www.openair.org

(guide to street markets, flea markets, farmers markets)

OrientalFood.com

www.orientalfood.com

(Internet site for Asian culture and food)

Pariscope

http://pariscope.fr

(Paris shopping, antiques, flea markets)

Pier 1 Imports, Inc.

800/245-4595 (for store locations)

www.pier1.com

(garden accessories and furniture, tableware)

Pottery Barn

800/922-5507 (for catalogue)

800/922-9934 (for store locations)

www.williams-sonoma.com

(garden accessories and furniture, tableware)

Provenance

1155 Foster Street

Atlanta, GA 30318

404/351-1217

(antiques, collectibles, tableware)

Restoration Hardware

415/924-1005 (for store locations)

www.restorationhardware.com

(garden supplies and houseware)

retro.modern.com

404/724-0093

www.retromodern.com

(Internet site for 20th-century design)

Ryan Gainey and Company

2793 Hardman Court NE

Atlanta, GA 30305

404/233-1805

(garden design, accessories and furniture)

Seeds of Change
888/762-4240
www.seedsofchange.com
(organic seeds, organic foods)

Select Seeds Antique Flowers
180 Stickney Hill Road
Union, CT 06076
860/684-9310 (for catalogue)
(vintage and heirloom seed varieties)

Shady Oaks Nursery
112 Tenth Avenue SE
Wascea, MN 56093
507/835-5033 (for catalogue)
(shady area plant specialists)

Smith & Hawken
800/776-3336
www.smith-hawken.com
(gardening supplies and clothes, plants, tableware)

Takashimaya, Inc.
693 Fifth Avenue
New York, NY 10012
800/753-2038 (for catalogue)
(bento boxes, Japanese tableware, flower shop)

Target Stores
800/800-8800 (for store locations)
www.target.com
(gardening supplies, kitchenware, tableware)

Tinder Box
888/827-0947 (for catalogue and store locations)
www.tinderbox.com
(fine tobacco products)

Tribeca Potters
443 Greenwich Street
New York, NY 10013
212/431-7631
(custom pottery)

W. Atlee Burpee & Company
300 Park Avenue
Warminster, PA 18974
800/888-1447
(bulbs, plants, seeds)

Weber-Stephen Products Company
3200 East Daniels
Palatine, IL 60067
800/446-1017
www.weberbbq.com
(Weber grills and grilling accessories)

Williams-Sonoma
800/541-2233 (for catalogue)
800/541-1262 (for store locations)
www.williams-sonoma.com
(garden accessories, furniture, kitchenware, tableware)

Wölffer Estate
Sagapond Vineyards
PO Box 9002
Sagaponack, NY 11962
516/537-5106
(verjus and fine wines)

World Variety Produce, Inc.
PO Box 21127
Los Angeles, CA 90021
800/588-0151
www.melissa.com
(dried and exotic fruits, grains, nuts)

Yard Co.
8430 Germantown Avenue
Philadelphia, PA 19118
215/247-3390
(ergonomic gardening tools, garden supplies)

Zabar's
2245 Broadway
New York, NY 10024
212/787-2000
800/697-6301 (for catalogue)
(gourmet foods)

Zona
97 Greene Street
New York, NY 10012
212/925-6750
(garden accessories, furniture, tableware)

I want to thank the Crevasse, Daubel, Harris, Schiebler, Lane and Faricy families who generously gave me access to their properties and gardens at Amelia Island Plantation. A heartfelt thanks to family friends Keith and Cindi Lane who were my resident guides to Amelia Island. I also want to thank Richard Goldman, Vice President of Marketing for Amelia Island Plantation, and the staff of The Amelia Island Club's Ocean Clubhouse for their hospitality and assistance ranging from bonfire building to allowing my crew unfettered access to this magnificent property. Working with Mumbo Jumbo's executive chef Shaun Doty continues to be an amazing experience. His modern culinary vision is full of joy, wonder and inspiration. Many thanks also to chef Nikki Cascone, whose eye for style and effervescent personality added sparkle to each day we worked together. To Brad Newton, photographer and friend, thank you for your relentless pursuit of light, color and the beautiful images on these pages. And to Jaroslav Kanka for his optimistic photographic assistance. Many, many thanks to superb designer Vivian Mize who worked by my side for long hours on countless occasions. I am thankful for her dedication to the visual identity of the *Modern* series. Kudos to Walter Reeves, a.k.a. broccoli boy, whose down-to-earth garden advice and sense of humor made even editing fun. I also want to thank writer Matthew De Galan for input and guidance. For keeping my temperamental computer and printers up and running, thank you, James Connor. I will always remember Tom Rutkowski with Arrington Aquatics for meeting me (and my mother) in the dead of winter in rural Florida with one perfect water lily. To Charles Smith at Cut Flowers in Atlanta and to Sara and Joe Edwards, proprietors of The Bird House on Amelia Island, thank you for glorious flowers. And to garden guru Ryan Gainey of Ryan Gainey and Company, thank you for the opportunity to photograph your personal garden, and for the wisdom you bestow so well. As always, thank you to the hardworking staff of Longstreet Press and to my editor, Suzanne De Galan. Lastly, thank you to my husband, Doug Sandberg — your support and love carry me beyond my dreams.

visit our web site at www.modernlifestyle.com